Mix and Match

by

Gordon Bailey

MIX and MATCH

This is the eighth published volume of the writings of Gordon Bailey, whose monologues and verses were brought to public attention in the 1960s by the actor Nigel Goodwin. Gordon's first book, *Plastic World,* published in 1971, sold many thousands in several editions. Requests are still being received for the use of republication of items from the first volume.

A pioneering work amongst pupils, offering them unconditional pastoral care and confidentiality, which Gordon began in the late 1950s, has led to the establishment of the work of the educational charity Schools Outreach. It is in aid of the work of this charity that this book is being offered for sale. The buyer can be assured that every penny of profit will go directly to the furtherance of this charitable work amongst deprived and disadvantaged children and young people.

Information about the work of Schools Outreach can be obtained by contacting the charity's head office in Worcestershire, England.

Schools Outreach
10 High Street
BROMSGROVE
Worcestershire B61 8HQ

Tel: 01527 574404
Fax: 01527 570321
e.mail: schools.outreach@mcmail.com

Mix and Match

A collection of jottings

by

Gordon Bailey

A SCHOOLS OUTREACH PUBLICATION

in paperback

Published by:
Schools Outreach Publications
10 High Street
BROMSGROVE
Worcs B61 8HQ

Printed and bound in Great Britain by:
A. J. Domone & Sons
7-9 Rowland Way
Hoo Farm Ind Est
Kidderminster
Worcs DY11 7RA

By the same writer:

Plastic World	1971	
Mothballed Religion	1972	
Patchwork Quill	1975	
Can a Man Change?	1979	
I want to tell you how I feel, God	1983	
100 Contemporary Christian Poets	1983	(Editor & contributor)
Stuff & Nonsense	1989	

INTRODUCTION

There follows a collection of bits and pieces, written over a number of years. Most of the contents of this book, though used in performance from time to time, have never been previously published. The book is a miscellany of offerings from amongst the material I refer to as my 'stuff'. I have had no particular pattern in mind as I've chosen the order in which pieces are placed. My hope is that this mix will provide you with the possibilty of matching the occasional verse to a mood in which you find yourself; a mood within which you wish for an opportunity to reflect, or feel a desire to be amused, or discover, during a moment in time, the need for a mental appetiser.

Some pieces were originally written for children and young people, being presented in a variety of settings, and always in a hope that a wee bit of implicit commonsense would take root.

Other pieces, especially, perhaps, the majority of my 'worsery rhymes', were written to do little more than create a smile or cause a laugh, though often the reaction proved to be a raised eyebrow followed by a groan.

I occasionally address myself to the Church, with tongue firmlly in my cheek, and once or twice do so on behalf of the young (who may have their tongues firmly sticking out!), believing that, as a commited member of our local parish church, I possess a somewhat more appropriate right to do so than those who adopt critical positions on the outside.

I hope that, as you read this mixture of my jottings, you will encounter some enjoyment.

Gordon Bailey
1999

CONTENTS

If only I could fly

The traffic's getting heavier,

the motorways are full;

the fumes are choking me to death;

I wish I was a gull!

Finn

Frederick Finn was terribly thin,

for he never took any goodness in.

He'd say his grace and admire the food,

but he wouldn't let it do him good.

His favourite read was the recipe book,

and he loved to watch his mother cook;

he liked the smell of her cakes and pies,

you should have seen the size of his eyes!

She'd see him smile at her mixing and beating,

yet never once did she see him eating.

Undernourished and underfed:

it has to be said that - Fred is dead!

Cigarette Smoker

'You do not smoke!' the wise man said,

addressing Tommy Tucker,

'It's the cigarette that does the smoking,

you are just the sucker.'

If

If we wish to communicate

on these few thoughts let's meditate:

avoid pretence, be real, be true,

that I might know who's really you.

Show me yourself in honesty,

not just the *you* you'd have me see.

We will not progress very far

unless you show me who you are.

Yet all is lost if you don't see

the person who is really me!

Little Miss

Little Muffet decided to rough it,

her present address? Cardboard City!

Said her dad: 'This life's rough';

said her mum: 'Had enough?';

but she wanted their love, not their pity.

Whether Map

There's weather today and there's weather tomorrow

and weather all over the globe;

there's weather with gladness and weather with sorrow,

and whether or not we should probe;

for

we analyse weather and forecast the weather

and whether by day or by night,

it seems people wonder, twixt thawing and thunder,

just whether we get weather right.

Ding

Ding dong bell

the apple looked real swell;

but the little boy's face was rosy red

so how did William Tell?

Mary

Mary had a little lamb,

it grew and grew and grew!

but later came to pieces

at a local Bar-B-Q.

Polly

Polly put the kettle on.

It suits you!

Together

Is living a matter of becoming or being?

Is learning dependent on looking or seeing?

Is loving assisted by listening or hearing?

Direction determined by motion or steering

Joy and fulfilment depend, I may find,

on using my eyes, and my ears, and my mind;

I'll learn that my wholeness depends upon whether

my eyes, ears, and mind have been working together.

Little Bo

Little Bo Peep has lost her sheep

and Humpty asked her why;

she said: 'Jack Horner's stolen them,

to put in his Christmas pie.'

Hickory Dickory Dock

Hickory dickory dock - the preacher watched the clock;

the clock struck one, he carried on - Hickory dickory dock.

Hickory dickory dock - the preacher forgot the clock;

the clock struck two, he wasn't through - Hickory dickory dock.

Hickory dickory dock - the people watched the clock;

the clock struck three, 'twas time for tea! - Hickory dickory dock.

Hickory dickory dock - a deacon watched the clock;

the clock struck four, they still got more - Hickory dickory dock.

Hickory dickory dock - the deacon stopped the clock ...

but he couldn't stop the preacher!

Apology 1

I am very sorry that our paperboy delivered to your home
a copy of 'Playboy' magazine instead of your usual 'Methodist Recorder'
I have, however, made a note of your comments
and will adjust your order accordingly.

Ding d...

Ding dong bell,

mummy's in the well;

but dad has thrown some quick lime down

so nobody can tell.

Desert Island Discus

One Shrove Tuesday

Robinson Crusoe tossed a pancake.

It landed on Friday.

Mary h..

Mary had a pretty nose,

it made her look quite stunning;

until the day she caught a cold

and couldn't stop it running.

Apartheid's Folly Exposed

Bar barred black man,

don't you dare come in,

sharing space with white folk

is a sin, sin, sin.

It's not that we detest you

and we've not been at the gin,

it's just that we think less of you

for reason of your skin.

Pussy foot

Pussy foot churchman, where have you been?

The service started at ten fifteen!

It's no use trying to make me think

you got here early but want a drink;

'cause I'm a vicar you won't beguile

by tip-toeing *backwards* down the aisle.

Thad

Thaddeus Thick was awfully sick

and wouldn't explain why he'd swallowed a brick;

then, later, said, with a foolish grin:

'I'm the sort of boy who'll take anything in.'

Jack

'Jack' said Jill, 'Is very ill,

and cannot stand the strain;

since falling down the hill he's got

some water on the brain.'

Ding do..

Ding dong bell,

another sunny spell!

The weather expert forecast rain...

ah, well.

The Grand ....

The grand old Duke of York,

he had ten thousand pimples;

he hired a drill, each one to kill,

replacing them with dimples.

Apology 2

I'm sorry I missed you last night;
I don't know how it happened.

I have, however, asked the maintenance men to immediately check
the trapeze.

Mary had

Mary had a little lamp to light her way to bed;

it should have helped the little scamp, but now our Mary's dead!

She lost her footing that dark night, she fell and now she's gone.

I wonder why, when she'd a light, she never turned it on.

Hair turned drey

Her eyes met mine,

our hearts entwined,

we kissed -

a real humdinger!

I ran my hands right through her hair

and a squirrel

bit my finger!

Dom

Dominic Drool truly thought he was cool

as he sniffed at the aerosol spray;

but only one breath was the cause of his death,

what a terrible price to pay.

Peer Pressure

'Here, Jill! said Jack, 'A twenty pack.'

said Jill: 'You must be joking.'

but by the time they'd made their climb

young Jill had started smoking.

First and last visit

Old ladies sneered at my pink shoes,

and frowned upon my girlfriend's trews;

The pastor nearly blew a fuse

while screaming out his long-held views

on dancing, cinemas, and booze,

on Roman Catholics and Jews;

he puzzled me, but gave no clues,

his sermon filled with donts and dos,

said nothing that was really news.

The organ never played the blues,

there were no ashtrays in the pews;

so now I know that, win or lose,

that church is not the place I'll choose

to spend my time on Sundays.

Naughty John

John was naughty, yet again,

his clothes were torn and muddy;

the teacher sent him, straight away,

to the headmaster's study.

He'd never had the cane before,

his terror proved a spur:

when told to touch his toes he said,

'We gonna play leapfrog, sir?'

Mary had a

Mary had a little nose

which grew, and grew, and grew;

until she couldn't reach it

when she blew, she blew, she blew.

Mary had a monstrous nose,

it really made her sick:

to blow her nose she had to put

her hanky on a stick!

Run rarebit run,

the cheese is overdone.

Mid Winter

Nights stay longer, days are shorter,

warm-wrapped skaters walk on water;

statuesque the swans have chosen

sheltered pools as yet unfrozen.

Stark against the snow the teasel's

darker than the Winter weasels;

skies are clear, the wind is bitter,

icing branches with its glitter.

Oak is naked, holly blushes;

moorhens tip-toe through the rushes;

tips of snowdrops now ascending,

heralding the Winter's ending.

Nat

Nathaniel Hird was a bit of a nerd,

who never listened to a word

of warning.

His ma and pa yelled 'Watch that car!',

but see his ashes in a jar

each morning.

Ding dong

Ding dong bell

I can never tell

the difference there is between

a dingle and a dell.

Apology 3

Darling,
I am <u>so</u> sorry that you discovered I have secretly been meeting someone else.
You must be heartbroken.
I feel it necessary to confess to you that I have had
several other affairs during our relationship.
Yours faithfully,

Grand old Duke

The grand old Duke of York

he had ten thousand feet;

his socks they filled a wardrobe

and went half way down the street.

Mary went

Mary went to hospital,

I do not mean to tease yer;

but when she had a little lamb

the midwife had a seizure.

Little Jack

Little Jack Horner sat in a corner

eating his Christmas pie;

he stuck in his thumb

and pulled out a drum,

and his mum said:

'O no, let me die!'

Pussy cat

Pussy cat, pussy cat, where have you been?

I booked a rail ticket to old Aberdeen.

Pussy cat, pussy cat, what did you there?

I never got further than old Euston Square!

They cancelled the train, which I think is criminal.

I'm feeling that waiting at Euston is terminal.

Ding dong b...

Ding dong bell,

it's awfully cold in hell:

you can't get near the fire for bishops.

Sapp

Simeon Sapp's in a bit of a flap,

as he dithers about what to do:

should he stay? Should he go?

Should he say 'Yes', or 'No'?

Should he choose to use plaster or glue?

For the choices in life he depends on his wife,

who has asked him to tile and to grout;

but Simeon Sapp's now a dim little chap,

'cause the light of his life has gone out.

What is?

What is the point of off'ring a joint

to one who has not started smoking?

For one who won't drag at the end of a fag

will be thinking the pusher is joking.

If you've already chosen to smoke by the dozen

(ignoring advice from your mother),

you'll probably make one more stupid mistake,

as one screw-up leads to another.

Apology 4

We are sorry that you have been receiving the Readers' Digest monthly magazine

despite your cancellations over the past eighteen months.

Thank you for reminding us yet again.

May I offer our profuse apologies.

We offer you a year's supply as compensation

and, as a regular reader,

you will naturally receive a 20% discount.

Ding dong bill

Ding dong bill,

pussy's very ill.

Give the moggy aspirin or

a paraceta-pill.

Colours

Reds and yellows in a jumble,

greys and golds and greenery;

make one's wondering senses tumble

by their restful unity.

Hues of amber, tones of blueness,

caught by sky and held by tree;

tinges changing, tints of newness:

Nature's potent therapy.

A couple of questions

Schoolboy: Please Miss,

should a person be punished for something he hasn't done?

Teacher: Of course not! Why?

Schoolboy: I haven't done my homework.

Counting

One, two, three, four, five,

too many people still alive.

six, seven, eight, nine, ten,

better go to war again!

The

The grand old Duke of York,

he had ten thousand pounds;

he spent it all on lions

which now roam around his grounds.

Apology 5

We are sorry you felt it necessary

to complain about the package holiday you booked with our company.

I assure you that no blame can attributed to us

for the fact that, when you arrived at the airport

from which you should have departed,

the aircraft was still unfinished.

Strange or what?

Some simple folk'll sit in their local

drinking down whisky and beer,

then follow a shandy with Baileys and brandy

and wonder why they feel so queer.

A what?!

Little Jack Horner sat in a corner

eating his Christmas pie;

he stuck in his thumb

and pulled out a double-decker bus

and said:

'I could've choked on that.'

A lake reflects

Take soft green trees and a Summer stirring,

unmelted snow in a mountain pass,

let a gentle breeze set the mixture blurring,

and serve in a silvered looking-glass.

Why?

Why are some churches derided,

and others decidedly odd?

Well, I've thought it through and decided

to pin the blame squarely on God.

He could have built churches of stone, slate, and pews,

with chancel, and turret, and steeple;

yet, with so much to choose, and so much to lose,

he went and made churches of people.

Little Bo Peep

Little Bo Peep has lost her sleep

and doesn't know what to do;

she's used to taking forty winks

each Sunday in the pew.

All the young folk used to nod

and no-one seemed to mind them;

but now the vicar's put his curate

in the pew behind them.

Apology 6

We are extremely sorry that the pet snake,

which you bought from us for your teenage son,

has swallowed your dog.

Our representative will call,

within the next 14 days,

and will look into things for you.

Jack and Jill went up the hill,

they climbed it higher and higher;

for every Sunday Jack and Jill

both sing in the High Church choir.

Beauty

Grace and beauty both existing,

set secure in rocks and ridges;

see the steadfast river twisting,

flowing free by wharfs and bridges;

vast, enduring, ever-pleasing,

life-sustaining loveliness,

all my wakened senses seizing,

stirring my perceptiveness.

Wondrous splendour, unconfined,

captivates and feeds my mind.

Good mourning!

I attended an odd but happy funeral today:

good grief!

There were four drunken bishops present:

good grasches!

There was one High Court judge:

good lord!

The vicar was a Welshman:

good Evans!

The dead man was Sir John Smith, philanthropist:

good knight!

The funeral, I was told, was cheap at the price:

good buy!

Winter to Spring

Nature shudders in her sleeping

as the waves of cold come creeping ...

ebb and flow.

Sunshine warms the trees to weeping,

frees the snowdrop, sets it peeping

from the snow.

Field poppy

Poppy-decorated silence,

through a sequence of Novembers;

note the fields in northern France

where Mother Nature too remembers.

Apology 7

We apologise for the inconvenience caused

when your holiday luggage

was confiscated on your return to this country.

Her Majesty's Customs Officials

are looking into your case.

X

X is a symbol for multiplication

X denotes my political choice

X is an illiterate person's signature

X is a request for anonymity

X means I got it wrong

Xmas?

Rector Rector

Rector, Rector, in you sector how do the churches grow?

With morning Mass, so Middle Class, and choirboys all in a row.

Vicar, Vicar, verger-picker, how is your church today?

With canticles and chiming bells and most folk staying away.

Member, Member, please remember, where is your burning zeal?

Now, was it doubt that put it out, or simply the way that you feel?

Mister, Miss, just think on this: God has a plan, you know,

it seems to me he'd like to see a garden of goodness grow.

He'd like your heart to play its part, he'd like his life in you.

Mary, Mary <u>was</u> contrary - but at least her garden grew!

Damien

Damien Dumm just sucks his thumb

and never listens to his mum,

who tries to tell him of life's dangers,

like taking lifts or sweets from strangers;

like poison berries and biting bugs;

or cigarettes, or harmful drugs;

like ignorance; or petty crime;

or carelessness; or wasting time;

like lack of trust; or selfishness;

or over-work; or under stress!

She warns him that such threats may come;

but Damien Dumm just sucks his thumb.

Wrong?

Ding bell dong -

I think I got that wrong.

Dong bell ding -

that's got a faulty ring.

Ding dong belt -

I think that that's mis-spelt.

Mary had a little lamb

Mary had a little lamb,

she offered it a cuppa;

later on she took it home

and ate it for her supper.

Match of the Day

Mankind is but a football in a game that's played by fools,

with no effective referee to emphasise the rules;

yet nailed upon a crossbar is a man, born for the role,

whom stupid men have put to death, refusing his control;

so, as a consequence, one finds an anarchistic game,

where death's a commonplace affair ... and no-one takes the blame.

Within the crowded stadium mankind gets kicked around;

his hopes and dreams and high ideals lie lifeless on the ground.

One commentator claims there isn't very long to play,

that most of those involved will be sent off on Final Day.

A starry universe spectates and wonders at a sport

where one must fill his pen with blood to write the match report.

MILK

There's sterilized, homogenized,

there's skimmed and there is pasteurized;

there's semi-skimmed, gold-top to savour;

there's strawberry and chocolate flavour;

there's milk from sheep, from cows, from goats;

there's warm milk on your porridge oats;

condensed milk and evaporated;

milk gone sour and milk that's dated;

milk in cartons, milk that's shaken;

milk delivered, milk that's taken;

milk in bottles, milk in jugs;

steaming milk in china mugs;

milk from powder, milk from breast;

I quite like milk - I bet you guessed!

Apology 8

Dear John and Helen,

We don't wish to alarm you, or spoil your holiday,

but we feel we ought to tell you that

the day after you left your little Jeremy with us

he swallowed my watch.

Mind you, it doesn't seem to be bothering him,

and he is passing time comfortably.

We shall, of course,

let you know the outcome.

Simon

Age of the Aquarist

My mind's a small aquarium where swims a school of thought;

a shoal of ever-new ideals, the slowly-moving sort,

which feed on meditation, neath an artificial light,

sustained within their little world all snug and watertight.

The water's warmed by faith and hope and gullibility,

while daydream-driven filters help remove reality;

a plastic-coated cover make quite sure they stay inside,

for the last ideal to leave my mind just flapped around - and died!

Some

Some wish to follow the road from Toronto,

though others may warn of its danger.

Some like the old-time film hero named Tonto,

whilst others prefer The Lone Ranger.

Many want Eucharist, incense, and steeple,

some churches have no such agendas.

Some folk watch 'Neighbours', or 'My Kind of People',

when others view only 'Eastenders'.

Some think church music sounds best from an organ,

while others would opt for guitar.

Some choose a Vauxhall, but others a Morgan,

when buying a second-hand car.

Some churches welcome new *blessings* for guidance,

when others remain more straitlaced.

How sad, is it not?, that the things which divide us

are largely a matter of taste.

So that's why!

Ding dong bell,

grandad's slippers smell;

that is why the pussy cat

is living down the well.

Q - What was the old Welsh miner's favourite hymn?

A - 'When the coal is hauled up Rhondda I'll be there'.

If only

If only he'd faced up to life as life is,
instead of inventing the lies;
if only he hadn't believed his own dreams,
if only he'd not fantasized;
if only he'd seen where his folly might lead,
if only he'd lifted the lid;
but he closed his mind to the truth he might find;
if only he'd not - but he did.

If only she'd questioned his motives that night,
if only she'd looked past his smile;
if only she'd dwelt on that glimmer of doubt,
if only she'd paused for a while;
if only she hadn't suppressed commonsense
when the eager young man made his bid,
she wouldn't be racked with regret and despair;
if only she'd not - but she did.

If only I hadn't have tried to assess
what I might achieve in return;
if only I'd offered myself to them both,
if only I'd showed some concern;
if only I'd not closed my eyes to their needs,
if I hadn't scamped and hid,
when I could have been of some help to my friends;
if only I'd not - but I did!

Jimmy knows

The teacher said to Jimmy, 'Will you listen now to me:

imagine you've a gun and there are twelve birds in a tree.

If you shot three, how many would be left? What do you say?'

Said Jimmy, 'You'd have three Miss,

you'd have scared the rest away!'

Apology?

I'm sorry that I feel I must

express this point of view:

'Society's professed concern is sham!'

For I'm judge quite completely

on the basis of I.Q.,

instead of on the basis of

'I am!'

My Testimony

(to be recited with
a very miserable facial expression
and an unhappy voice)

Let me tell you about my church, or is it 'citadel'?
Or 'mission'? No! Or 'chapel'? No! Assembly? No! Oh well:
I haven't been a member long - well, 'member' so to speak;
see, what I mean by 'member' is I go there once a week.

I'd never been to church before, not since my niece was christened,
and made no sense of what went on, despite the fact I'd listened.
Mind, during 't vicar's solemn prayer we'd all had quite a laugh,
he'd pulled the plug from out the font, which gurgled like a bath!

Still, back to what I want to say: I go each Sunday night,
and have done ever since the time they say I 'saw the light'.
A preacher'd come and said 'Get saved!', no, wasn't Billy thingy,
he'd said 'The world's a sinking ship and Jesus is our dinghy.'
He'd urged us all to climb aboard, I thought, 'This fella's daft,
to leave the world behind you need a rocket not a raft!'
He begged for folks to raise their hands, he really pleaded hard;
I lifted mine and, quick as wink, I had my Union Card.

Ever since folks shake my hand and call me 'brother', s'true;
at first they'd come and sit with me and show me what to do.
They taught me how to keep myself from shouting 'Praise the Lord!',
explaining that such things occur, but usually abroad.
I had to learn just when to stand, and when to bend my knees,
I had to learn a whole new language, filled with thous and thees;
I had to learn to sing the hymns, and listen to the choir,
I had to learn to find my way from Jude to Obadiah.

At first I found it pretty tough but, now, I'm glad to say,
I know most of the choruses, and even how to pray.
And when they pass the plate, so I can put my twenty p in,
I've even learned to do it now without the others seein'.

It's quite a place, so warm and friendly, all the chairs are new,
we sit each Sunday evening waiting, praying just for you.
So why not pay our church a visit, all the seats are free,
I'm certain you'd enjoy yourself - there's lots of folks like me!

Sol

He, the source of life, offers direction,

Lord of day and, sometimes, by reflection,

serves the night; or gives the storm a rainbow.

He, the Light, provides all health and growing,

sheds his warmth to thaw all coldness; throwing

shadows, glowing soft within his halo.

He, the spring of energy, emerging

fresh with dawn to set our spirits surging.

Enlightened, we behold what he has done

and, opening wide our lives, welcome the Son.

Sunset

Clouds made soft by black swan's feathers

give the blood-red orb its pillow;

gentle evening zephyr gathers

wisps of blue, of grey, of yellow;

waves the poplars for his brushes,

washes dusk with variegation,

wafts the clouds to cool their blushes,

hallows sun with coronation,

splashes gold in every quarter,

silhouettes the night owl's flying,

ripples crimson on the water.

Who would think that day is dying?

John 14.6.

Christ is the Way that Life makes sense,

for he is the Truth in the present tense.

Think about it!

GOD is GOOD with nothing taken away

GOOD is GOD with nothing added